Mindful Thoughts

A Book of Poems

MARIO GIVENS

Mindful Thoughts

@Copyright 2017 by Mario Givens

All rights reserved. No part of this book maybe reproduced or transmitted in any form or by any means without written permission from the author.

Printed in the United States of America

Foreword

Author Mario Givens will showcase poetry in different ways to capture the audience with his words, phrases, and symbolism to tell a story. In this book, each selections of poems will connect his thoughts to his audience, so they can grasp a vision like no other.

This book, *the Mindful Thoughts* will continue to hold you speechless and will make you feel closer to the author. Just visualize yourself in the authors thoughts and take a journey to mental peace.

Dedication

This book is dedicated to my late grandma because she was my inspiration and she motivated me more after she saw my first book The Love Notes. My grandmother passed away right after I showed her my dream as an author came true and her telling me she was proud of me. My grandmother discussed with me that when she was growing up she was a poetry writer and she always wanted to become an author. I told her that my next book will be dedicated to her because she never had an opportunity to have a book. This book will have a total of 93 poems because that was the age when she passed away. Rest in Peace Susie Jean Givens, I will always miss you and love you.

Introduction

Mindful Thoughts, is a poetry book that comes from a place of gratitude, sincerity, humbleness, and honesty. This book takes the reader on a journey that consist of Love, hope, and awareness to love. I want the readers to grasp from the versatility that the author showcases and the different genres from each poem. These poems are events that I capture throughout my life and all the poems are created by me the author.

Table of Contents

Foreword iii
Dedication v
Introduction vi
Sunshine 1
Walk of Destiny 3
A Deadly Day 4
I'm Thankful 5
Rainstorm 6
The Stars 7
Face to Face with a Angel 8
A Tender Sound 10
Death to Hate and Those Who are Apart 12
Knock Knock 14
A Look Back in Time 15
Hugging My Son 17
Massage 18
A+ 20
Adore 22
Woman 23
A Kite that Flies 26
Through it All 26
A Flight to Live 28
Special Day 29
Visual Clarity 31
Royal Angel 32
Forecast 34
Grammatical Pain 36
Friendship 38
Her Eyes 39
Picture Perfect 41

Carnival	43
God Listens	44
No Comparisons	45
She's Beautiful	47
My Friend	49
So Smooth	51
Simple Friendship	53
Mother's Day	54
Need a Umbrella	56
Perfection	57
Weather Report	59
Passion	61
Anxiety	62
English	64
Books (people)	66
Forever Memories	68
4 wings	70
A Second to Think	72
Beginning of Love	73
A Friend Request	75
Next Door Angel	78
Peace Anticipation	80
Ultimate Love Making	83
English Creates Love	85
Anxious for Love	87
Beautiful Morning	88
Slow dance	89
Hurt but Still Love	90
Calm	91
O'clock	92
I Miss You	94
Questions	95
Universe Don't Lie	96
A shower of peace	98
Free from Hurt	99
A Thought in the Garden	100
A Nice Horseback Ride	101

Truthful skies	103
Motivating Tulips	104
Inspiring Good Morning	105
Air	106
A Day of Hurt	107
Love Died	108
Silent destiny	109
Hello	110
Galaxy of Clarity	111
A Careful Gift	112
A Perfect Creation	113
Mysterious Thoughts	114
You Are Everywhere	116
Forbidden Love	117
Ocean	119
Fallen Leaves	120
Thoughts	121
Orchids	122
Forever Queen	123
Sacred Dinner	124
Tears for Mama	126
A Dateless Day	128
Sheltered Hurt	129
Scarred Love	130
A Praying Star	131
Happier Feeling	132
Cupids Arrow	133
Appreciation and Gratefulness	135

Mario Givens

Sunshine

It was a bright moment

I capture her glow

She makes life easier

Hers rays always show

She's so beautiful

A smile of joy

I respect her

Appreciate the brightness she brings to me

A breath of fresh air

The trees talk to the leaves

Her rays are shining

The squirrels are out to play

The calmness from her eyes

It's just a wonderful day

A moment to cherish

The warmth is cool

Thoughts of happiness

As the pigeons slowly flew

Mindful Thoughts

It's a day to remember

Can't wait to see her soon

A kiss goodbye

The sunsets

Now here comes the moon.

Mario Givens

Walk of Destiny

Take this walk with me

Hold my hand of sincerity

I really enjoy your time

The moments we share

Happiness guides us

Lead us to freedom

To a place of love

A destination of care

We decided to stop and embrace it

Love found us

When we chose to accept it.

A Deadly Day

It was a gloomy day

The temperature was cool

The hearts were cold

Why do this happen?

What can we do to change it?

We all are tired

Can we escape this punishment?

Too many souls die

Their spirits weren't pure.

Mario Givens

I'm Thankful

Thank you for your heart

The opportunity to be happy

The days I'm sad

I thank you

You made me stronger

Pain didn't last longer

I'm grateful

Our moments were amazing

You shared

I shared

We were identical

I'm sincere

Your ability to make me better

I became a man

Even my failures are gains

I know my worth

Do you accept my gratitude?

Rainstorm

The rain tells so many stories

The pain and hurt

Sometimes the glory

It relaxes the brain

Creates a mental space

The euphoria sneaks in

Calms the place

A puddle begins

Each drop has a reason

Whenever it rains

A different chapter brings a season

It defines serenity

The drops hitting the earth

It brings tranquility.

Mario Givens

The Stars

As you sit in the sky

I visualize freedom

Attach to the universe

The moon gives you a wink

You like the security of the night

Allowing the light to glow

Scattered

The dreams of the dark

A planet that shines

Revolution of the evening.

Face to Face with a Angel

A dream

A wonderful night

A glamour of a comet

An anxious scream inside

Wow she's here

A face of glow

A queen of wisdom

A lonely fish

Inside my eyes

Wow again

I can't believe

This opportunity

An honor

A moment of true

The nerves I have

Heart beating

What should I do

This is a dream

A woman

A crush

A high school sweetheart

Without her knowing

Eyes of grace

A walk that had me

Vision a princess

That has a mental crown

That one day I can bow to her throne.

A Tender Sound

That voice

So poise

So soft

A whisper inside of noise

Like a peace rally

With words of grace

That voice

Lips that pronounce verbs when you say

Hey baby

Thanks sweetie

Adverbs

When you need me

That voice

That relaxes depression

That soothes me

A rhythm of perfection

Mario Givens

This voice

Brings me to joy

A conversation of peace

A silent night

With romance when you speak.

Death to Hate and Those Who are Apart

These souls are fraud

The sinners in flesh

Disrespected god

The judgment of fallers

The ones who create hate in others

The demons in clothes

Your mothers, sisters, friends, lovers and brothers

They all sin

They all have flames in their eyes

So addictive

To the opportunity drive

No shame

It disgusts my heart

The bleeding inside

From their hatred spark.

What goes around

It will be back in threes

The death of hate, unconscious, the need of opportunity.

These are real tears

They only run through my veins

Sadness of love ones

The price for not using your brain

Misery loves friends

So you all can live as one

The leeches of the earth

The suicide from ignorance of your mental gun.

Knock Knock

Sitting here biting my nails

Wondering why I left

Did I make a mistake?

Create a space

Loneliness invades my heart

Is it too late

I'm distant

Determine

Grateful for the moments

The memories I adore

Can love be no more

Did the door close on us

You need to knock

That when I answer

Your heart will drop

Welcome home

To a new life without regrets.

A Look Back in Time

I wish I had a time capsule

I would bring back your smile

The feelings when I was a child

My love for you is sincere

I'm a servant to you

Please speak to me

Create a voice reasoning

A dialogue of truth

I miss you

An empty heart

My angel took a vacation

Why did you go?

I didn't say goodbye

All I have is my cries

Mindful Thoughts

A face full of water

I need you

My umbrella to this storm

A thought of a forehead kiss

My past I have you

My present you gone

My future you will be miss.

Hugging My Son

You are me

A reflection from a star

I'm proud to be your dad

Honor to be a leader

A student of God

Grateful I can hug you

Tell you I love you

Appreciate that you listen

I will never turn my back

I'm in front

Motivating

Inspiring

Showing you a man

I hope you understand

I pray you stay humble

Your journey will come

I can't wait to pass you my crown

A king is born.

Massage

My eyes are close

I'm the man you chose

Hands on your soul

I'm so bold

As your back fold.

I relax you

Got you having dreams

That seem true

That state of mind

The reasons you blind

So you can feel calm

Feel like a day of peace

A warm bath

Your body at ease.

These oils run down

Filling all your skin

While my soft lips

Mario Givens

In your ear

Whispering.

Moaning

Telling you I love

I care

I need

So when you open your eyes

I'll be the MAN you see.

My hands strong

Your body soft

My truth not wrong

Our love has no faults.

A+

A piece of art

A place to showcase your beauty

A time to calculate how much you care

An hour thinking about me

A reason to be happy

An honor to believe in me

A moment to respect

A future for us

A heart that beats

A soul full of trust

A mind full of ideas

A topic that don't consist of hate

A woman that knows

A lady that have inside sexiness that shows

A consistent relationship

A night of passion

A day wondering if he's a has been

A dream full of smiles

A nightmare on times I was wild

A song that has your ears hearing joy

A voice screaming love

A separation between man and boy

A bed full of love making

A bath full of warmth

A morning full of hoping

A lifetime with my infinite token.

Adore

The wind blew you my way

I'm relax from your aura

I want your presence to stay

I desire your heart

Your soul is full of devotion

The dedication you have for love

A thought of romance

I'm addicted to your potion

You have so much passion

I'm infatuated by your grace

The amatory of your spirit

Venus is the Ultimate place.

Woman

You can have what you need

The goal

A man on his knees

Praising your soul

While he bows down to your feet

Power of woman

We cherish your mind

The independence of your persona

The strength that comes from your spine.

It's you

The woman

That captures our weak side

The hardness from our hands

Shakes without you on our side

The woman

The person who holds us down

A beautiful understanding of god

A sunshine in that all white gown.

The woman

Mindful Thoughts

The most powerful noun on this earth

She can stop wars

It's not hard to figure her worth.

She wants a king

She wants to groom that prince

That way when he's around her

The relationship makes since.

This woman is so strong

He's in the kitchen cooking dinner

He's running bath water

He wants to be the winner

He wants her heart to be the trophy

Their status is champions

50/50 was the glory.

The woman

Let me say again

The woman

The one who can walk pass

The smell of fragrance

A smile that makes us shine

The walking rays of light

You came into our dark lives

Now our spirits are bright.

The woman

That brings the Shakespeare out of us

The poetry when we are inside you

The rhymes of love are our trust.

This woman is close

Some under our nose

We got some on our arms

Just respect the ones we chose.

A Kite that Flies Through it All

I'm at peace

My mental at ease

Just free

It's good to be me

Full of flaws

A life of cause

I guess imp true

So loyal

Honest with my feelings

Now I know what to do.

Just staring

Wishing it was me

Letting the positivity

I call it wind

That blows me away

From the bad

The sad

Take me to the tree full of glad.

The breeze so calm

The sun is my mind

So away from the moon

That completes the night

With the love

That represent light

That penetrates life.

I want to be held

Never let me blow to evil

Conquer this moment

Frame this

So ecstatic

As I sit.

Many days I can't fly

Many days I fall

Get wet

The puddle is the barrier

That challenge my world

The thunder shakes me

Have to go in because

The lightening can strike

mood.

A Flight to Live

I'm free

Distant from negativity

I became a bird

I can fly to happiness

Soar to a place of peace

Determine to land on positivity.

Special Day

The grass

Is where I lay

Thinking

Hoping

Praying for you.

the breeze chills my soul

Takes the warmth

Creates a guard

From the cold heart.

I can hear the ocean

Telling me you still care

That our love was rare

So sacred to truth

As the gulls flew

Telling me this what I should do

Take your hand

Look in your eyes

Cry with joy.

Mindful Thoughts

Feelings that can't be disguise.

Take that walk

Enjoy the sand through our toes

Who knows

What the fish may think

What the whales would say

As the dolphins play.

The sun wink with praise

The clouds so soft

They just stayed

Picking up rocks

Take a short throw

They skip across the water

Like your soul skip

Across that part

Finally, it stops

That right place

My heart.

The wind

Got the leaves cheering

God creations are

Enjoying our special day.

Visual Clarity

Have you ever made love?

Gave peace into another

With each kiss

Your hands create visions

You hold tight

Mesmerizing in your eyes

Ecstasy on every sight

Your kisses hold passions

It activates my chakras

Enlighten my pineal

An erotic feeling

I find myself deep inside words

You so beautiful

But those kisses captured me

The energy

Chemistry

A reflection of Gods thoughts

She's the flower that blossom

Into a dream of pecks.

Royal Angel

It's one thing to be so beautiful

Then your spirit is mutual

Amazing

Angelic Queen

I can see her wings when she walks

Since of ease when she talks

A vision of royalty

She wears her crown well

So I bow my head

Humble myself when I'm in her presence

Submit to her heart

She deserves the best

I can see her greatness

How can a king speak?

Explain his goals

His roles

When she has a kingdom

Mario Givens

I close my eyes

Create a relationship

In my dream

She captures my eyes

A nice picnic

Will be her surprise

Wine

Sunshine

Her smile

Makes the waves of the lake move

Her eyes keen like the birds that fly

As she passes by

Her scent is like flowers grew fresh in the yard

I'll play my part

Stay in my lane

Until we together in the dark

My eyes close

Time to be with you in my dream again.

Forecast

It was like a classic movie

I took you on a date

Walk you down the beach

As you listen to the words I say

You on my mind

Why you cross my thoughts

Trying to remind speechless

So I stay quiet

Don't want rejection to conquer my heart

But I continue to be true

Staying humble

Grateful that I talk to you

It's not a dream

More like peace through words

My body melts

When I see that face

Put me in another place

Like Venus

Mario Givens

The planet of love

Or maybe an angel

a dove that flies above

Just a quick reminder

Just wanted you to know

Whenever you get free time

The weather permits

I'll take you on that walk

But until then we stuck with the snow.

Grammatical Pain

Pain made love to happiness

Created confusion

Illusion

Lust created temptation

Content

Comfortable

Communication died

Separation of hearts

Alone in an empty space

All you have is your thoughts

Loyalty disrespects resentment

Every word said in your head

A comma kisses

The question marks

Exclamation marks is furious with quotations

So I continue to think

Internally speak

Visualizing a euphoria

Mario Givens

A scent from passion

Destiny divides day dreams

Sadness was a past tense

A completion of peace

When soul makes love to spirit.

Friendship

You are my friend

A support system

I dedicate my time to you

My advocate

Your advice is true

I benefit from being acquainted

You are more than an associate

My consultant

We collaborate on honesty

Only competition comes from who loves who more.

Her Eyes

I can see them

They have fire in them

They scare me

I don't know what to think

I feel as though you want me

The color inside

The rainbow of pride

The loyalty I know you have

I can feel it

Why they are doing that

Moving around

With wisdom of care

I love you too

Too bad I can't kiss them

Hold them

But I can take them places

Only they want to go

Mindful Thoughts

As they are going down my body
Finding all my soft spots
Damn I'm getting hot
I can't hurt you
I scared of the wet drops.

Mario Givens

Picture Perfect

It was a calm and relaxing day

You made my night peaceful

I'm happy you flew across my world

An angel without wings

Your smile makes the sun jealous

When you walk the birds chirp

The butterflies sit on your shoulder

You are a gift from God

A surprise to my heart

My soul relaxes when you speak

Your voice is like a melody

I'm lost in your eyes

They told a story of trust

I can't wait to take walk on the beach

The blue ocean of Puerto Rico

Your skin is like the sand

I'm mesmerized by your spirit

Mindful Thoughts

When Nightfall comes

I'll miss your aura

Hopefully I can see this picture again.

Mario Givens

Carnival

It's a warm sunny day

We take some hours to have fun

Paid our admission

Teddy bears will be one

Amusement park love

All we see is laughter

Clowns with balloons

We stop at an exhibit

I'm so glad we visit

A lot of festivities

Many things to do

People in masquerade costumes

Then we stop to eat

Feeding each other fruits

We are getting closer to night

The fireworks begin to show

Sitting in the grass

Cuddling with love

The colors brighten the sky

A perfect date before we go

God Listens

Only God knows my hurt
The pain inside my heart
Only God knows my intentions
The confusion of my thoughts
Only God knows my struggle
The battle with my illness
Only God knows my strength
The ability to motivate others
Only God knows my weakness
The inability to stay focus
Only God knows my smile
The reasons to make others happy
Only God knows my future
He created me, and he created my eternity.

No Comparisons

She can say she loves you

I'm the one she sees

She can give you a warm hug

I'm the one she feels

The nights in bed

I'm the one who she wants

My soul will always haunt

No matter what you do

My spirit flows through her mind

I taught her feelings

Real love is never blind

I'm the one who knows

Every secret that's hiding

Ask the questions

The answers are not hard to find

Listen to her voice

The truth is never lying

Mindful Thoughts

The devil has feelings

They say lust

I hold all the keys

To unlock the doors of trust

Enjoy your days

Nights I'm inside her dreams

As she wakes from a nightmare

A vision of me makes her inner scream

Things that feel good, that's a short-term goal

I'm a lifetime token

Clean, smooth as gold

I got things to offer

A man with worth

That perfect love song

No cries, deceit, or hurt.

Mario Givens

She's Beautiful

Bright

Like the sun during the day

She beautiful

The moon contacted the stars

And requested love

She's that beautiful

So beautiful that I can hold her in my dreams

Make love to her screams

Let her eyes penetrate my heart

Go so deep into my soul

With lips of cushion

Body of a goddess

She's so modest

I can relax my head on her ideas

She that's beautiful

So beautiful

I can kiss her hand

Mindful Thoughts

Let my reasons expand to truth

What a man to do

Hold my feelings

release my passion into her world.

Respect her decisions

Stay loyal to her happiness

As she rubs my head

Protect my emotions with her spiritual sword

Craving for more

Depending on her

The backbone of my life.

Mario Givens

My Friend

Another soul

This one was close

These tears stood still to my cheek

My emotions are worse

My hands shook with fear

Confuse on his state

What was he thinking

A friend didn't wake

Why take him

He changed for the best

A smile of peace

He took the positive test

It really hurts

Now the tears roll down

A king left the throne

The memories are the crown

I need to wake up

This dream needs to end

Mindful Thoughts

As my eyes are soak
My pain bleeds this pen.
A bullet shouldn't decide
Your fate was REAL
This man had heart
A prayer for the love ones
A moment to heal.
The tears make puddles
Every time I think
I'll never forget you
If I blink
Focus on your new journey
We will meet again
Another one gone
Peaceful tears for a special friend.

So Smooth

So smooth

Got my heart smiling

Got my veins blushing

From the thought of your love

You are smooth

The look in your eyes

The lips of different worlds

Made me want to come close

To taste your passion

To hold your body

The pillow of love

The skin of ivory

With a pinch of essence

So smooth

I wonder your thoughts

A quick moment of convo

Mindful Thoughts

Had my brain call my mind
This is the woman
That my wisdom found
That my understanding search for
My knowledge hope for
I wonder Mrs. smooth
Do you feel the same?
Reverse these words
Like if you were saying.

Simple Friendship

It felt good

Your support

You saw my vision

Executed my mission

My goal was true

My heart was real

now my soul knows what to do.

Thanks

My mind adopted you

My gut honor you

You are my friend

My lifetime token

The reason I smile

The loyalty

The respect I have

I Wish you will advise me more.

Mother's Day

She Nourish

The teacher of the Earth

The motivator

The emotional speaker

I love you

From the wisdom of your words

To the paradise of your love

You taught me life

The man I am today

I listen

Even when the anger gets in my way

I love you

The times you taught me math

English frustrated my mind

You said never give up

That spanking not too far from behind

The times we were poor

You made meals from your soul

The clothes were clean

The house was perfect

elegance of your beauty

The vision through the religion of God

You made us close

Made us understand family

The meaning of failure

Let us know that success will not come easy

So I'm blessed to be your lifetime servant.

Need an Umbrella

The rain drops making beats against the window

As my nature creating a rhythm inside your lyrics

The rain stops

Giving us the time to hear it

A song of moans

Your kisses be the chorus

The rain starts again

Craving for more

The harmony

The pitch of your voice

Wet from your moist

Your body is flooding

Making a puddle

A lake

Now your waves are against my land

Bringing out a rainbow

When we both hit our peeks

The soothing words of I Love You as we speak.

stop thinking so much.

Perfection

No eyes could see

No ears could hear

A sight of volume

Master of paradise is near

Truly beautiful

I can't define

Secure my WORTH

Execute my love

You complete me

I desire you

The passion of truth

No lies

I benefit from honesty

Some days it hurts

All nights I'm alone

These tears

Replace lakes

As lakes replace oceans

Mindful Thoughts

I cry every day.

You told me it will get better

I see the sun losing shine

As the moon becomes blind

My world ends.

Mario Givens

Weather Report

They want your happiness

That romance

The extra night

With passion of massages

An hour of foot rubs

Soak your body in my heart

That moment of truth

The cries that gets wipe clear from my lips

That's love

That's what grandma had

Making love to the rain

So every time a drop fall

I go deep inside your earth soil

Every time it thunders

You scream with ecstasy

As my lightning bolt strikes Your trees

It's a storm

A hurricane

Mindful Thoughts

This tornado twirls until I destroy the tense in your body

Now you can relax

Sleeping peacefully as the storm passes.

Mario Givens

Passion

Like wishing

Without a genie

Without the backbone

Next to me

I want you

I need that

The moment of memories

Want it back

I'm too strong

Full of passion

Waiting to empty this heart

Fulfill you with romance

A classic love movie

As your sex moves me

I can cum off your looks

Damn you that fine

I'll stay alone

Until your fire burn

And decide to love my life.

Anxiety

It's times where I want to take a ride

Get away from the world

Often, I want to hide

Then I realize

Life is not that that hard

Running away from my fears

I'm nervous to live

Afraid of my trials

I need to understand my tribulations

Life is not that hard

It's so much tension

Too much worrying and wishing

My thoughts are uneasy

My neck begins to get tight

I don't have no sense of security

Life is not that hard

Mario Givens

Where can I get some calm?

There's no need to panic

Those attacks can be distracted

Hopefully I can find some peace

Tranquility finally became me

Life is not that hard.

English

Absence makes the heart lonely

I can feel the ice in my blood

No one to love

No soul to hug

A mind without a dove

A reason to search

An opportunity to find

Where are you

Come inside this web

Capture your body

Create a mental family

You are my world

The passion of trying

The ultimate communication

You are my life

That infinite charm

I whisper my feelings

Your ears are having an orgasm

Mario Givens

Your eyes are wet with joy

I made love with my words

Create a sentence with verbs

Let me teach

Become your answers

To your lifetime of questions.

Books (people)

A moment has come

Thoughts fights emotions

I see you when you pass

You leave a scent

Thoughts again

The past I don't resent

I'm focus on the present

But we are distant

Distracted by the assumptions

But God's gift brought our words together

A verb replaces a noun

An opportunity to smile

Discuss the future

I'm a book with a unique style

Pick me up and read

Understand me

Proofread me

So when you put me back on the shelf

Mario Givens

I'm here if you need me

Because the words inside me

Will show you that the book you pick up

Was a good read.

Forever Memories

You are my angel

My heart kisses your heart

With ever beat

I don't want to let go

It's more than a bond

You are my halo

My spirit flies free

With every flow of your wings

God has a new friend

In His garden

He plants 6 flowers

That only you can water

So we all can be great

Every drop is your soul

Teaching us to have faith

Then Leave a legacy

Be what you meant to be

It's days and nights I don't know what to do

My angel continues to fly over me

So when I see a butterfly

I will no longer be confused

My love for you is true

It hurts that you not here

I sincerely miss, and I will always love you.

4 Wings

Devastating

Only good can come from this

Lessons learned

Souls will be miss

It's a time to pray

A second to believe

Angels being call

Gods soldiers of deeds

It's going to hurt

The pain will remain here

Reasons of peace

With every dropping tear

God heals all wounds

Their wings flap with love

4 graceful soars

Peaceful Like doves

They can hear the calls

The words of help

Mario Givens

Mom we love you

Their spirits we felt

Heaven has 4 wings

The grass is green

Gods sits at throne

Eternity of kings and queens.

A Second to Think

It's like you looking

But what do you see

A vision of greatness

Longevity

What are you thinking

Do you want to take that chance?

The ability to have romance

Swept off your feet

Wine and dine

That's all fine

I wish and pray you achieve

I hope the main thought you are having

Is having those memories with me.

Mario Givens

Beginning of Love

Sometimes I worry

Get confuse

I want things in a hurry

Anxious

I don't want to lose

So I stay patient

But can't lie it's hard

When you want something

So bad

It just seems so far

What should I do

I express

Confess

Don't want to be a fool

Should I fall back

Allowed a dream to consume me

What is it about her

Why do I feel this way?

Mindful Thoughts

Why can't she take a chance?

See it's more than romance

It's a friend

A partner

Opportunity to build

Old school courting

You know

What's your favorite color

Favorite food

Do you like me

Circle yes

But if you say no

At least I tried

But I have my moments

I'll take my time

Hopefully the wait is great

Like the taste of wine.

A Friend Request

I vision you

The night I requested you

I was nervous

Didn't know if you would accept

So I kept scrolling

Hoping

Wishing

I didn't pray

But I did say

Accept

Because I saw you

I noticed your eyes

They were at peace

Telling stories

The personal mysteries

Then I see you accept

A smile from ear to ear

So I look at your face

Mindful Thoughts

It was like an angel

Your wings later were your inner strength

Your soulful gift

But back to that face

So pretty

Beauty is her name

Lips like a queen who demands respect

Skin from the clay that God form

Then you appear

With so many qualities

Release the fear

Let go of the anxiousness

I'm a good listener

Your words I hear

So I keep looking

Found my favorite picture

It captures my mind

Then I got sick

Before I could say hi

Then you appear with encouraging words

You made my night

Like the moon in the sky

You more than beauty

You are a walking paragraph

The chapters you speak of

Like my sentences

So I pray

One day

When you turn your page

You will be free

Destined

To complete your journey.

Next Door Angel

She has her king

He sits next to her wings

This angel of my eyes

Your mind completes me.

Your presence demand love

Your heart full of joy

The warmth of your soul

The ice on your lips

Body heat that melts the cold.

Look at you

You can brighten the night

Many stars get jealous

Your beauty

Represents the light.

Mysterious woman

Can I read your lines?

Use your body as my canvas

Create a portrait

I need to handle this.

My queen

Oh, hail my queen

So sexual with your king

Need my mouth in between

These strange things

As your lust

Confuse me.

Look me in my eyes

Tell me you need me

Make lifetime decisions

A life of royalty.

Peace Anticipation

My demise

The day will come

The preparation of a prophet

Creating a mindset

The last days was fun.

I have so much to offer

Many feel my pain

Talk through the souls

The ones who feel the same.

My heart is strong

Sometimes my brain gets jealous

They both fight for right

To defend my trust.

I believe in the world

Some days God tells me it's okay

I ask for strength

On my knees

Head touching the floor

Mario Givens

5 times a day I pray.

My demise

The preparation of a prophet

The messenger of truth

The reason I fight battles

The warrior I be

The fight for honesty

That reside in me.

I want to be a legend

I'm considered a king

The throne I stand on

The spiritual words I bring.

My time will come

I'm not scared of it

I need my love ones

To see my thoughts are real

A puddle of knowledge

As my understanding spills.

Some say he's crazy

Others feel my path

Not the same years ago

Those chapters I have pass.

Mindful Thoughts

I let few get close

Others my guard is up

That doesn't mean no love

Just a question mark by your trust.

Embrace what you get

Who say another will come

Listen to trees

The lakes and oceans have something to say

God creations have meanings

Take responsibility for what he made.

Ultimate Love Making

I waited

Anticipated

The thoughts of me putting my love inside you

So when you release your energy

My connection is positive

But I got to give

more

Secure my emotions

So I won't confuse love from lust

Because this was more than a bust

I injected my trust

You receive a dosage

That way every ejaculation has a meaning

A purpose

Longevity

Souls surface

Earths move

Clouds pause

Mindful Thoughts

Rain pours

I got to give MORE

Create a fire

Eliminate a desire

But implement a NEED

So the want is minimum

Every touch is passionate

Not venom

You can look inside my eyes

The words I LOVE YOU

Will thrust

When God allow the earth to beat.

English Creates Love

She knows

I sent the words

I express the verbs

Created many verses

Use command to add how I feel

Question marks to wonder why

Quotations so she knows I'm honest

Exclamation points when I'm excited about her

I wrote so much

Because I love so much

That it hurts

God this is who I want

Who I need

What more do I have to do

Do I deserve her

Worthy of her

She's my book

My chapters

Paragraph of love

She keeps breaking my heart

She ends it with a period.

Mario Givens

Anxious for Love

In my thoughts

I'm guided by wishes and hopes

Finding myself anxious

Meditating to cope

She always captures my eyes

What you see?

A Queen

Her crown controls my heart

Submissive to her words

I kneeled before her

Kiss her hand and feet

Then I bow to her

Letting her know she can trust me

But the distance between her throne and mines

Keeps the kingdom silent

But I feel her energy

Producing waves in my chakras

I'm control by the universe

Beautiful Morning

A morning sip of tea

It's starts my day off

Then she walks in the kitchen

My heart beats so soft

She attracts my eyes to her beauty

I pour her a cup of coffee

A king and Queen

That's how it should be

It's a day of peace

More thoughts of she

Her soul is pure of love

She caters to my life

I'm motivated to love her

Inspired to do right

I have a few more hours to adore her

Before the moon bless the night.

Slow Dance

You are a reflection

Perfection

A moment to grasp

My breath blows away

I'm caught up in your smile

Your eyes penetrate my eyes

I see clear

Here is where you stay

I take your hand

Passion passes into your hand

Romance kisses your spirit

Can I have this dance?

Hurt but Still Love

It was a moment

She creates a vision of me

Then her vision was blurry

She's distracted by love

Disrupted by hurt

The pain over power her

She's alone

Safe inside her feelings

The trust is gone

Men were wrong

Devastated by the swarm

Her soul crashes

She's in pieces

Shattered by dreams

Forever screams

She needs peace

Emotions needs a vacation

Her destination, Holy matrimony.

Calm

A warm afternoon

The birds chirping

The bees create honey

The earth is replenished

The flowers blossom

A quiet breeze

The trees talk

Squirrels collects food

A perfect day for a walk.

O'clock

Time is ticking

It never stops

It has no destination

Tick tock

She's not here

Where is she

Will she come to me?

I'm lonely

Anxious

The clock strikes again

Tick tock

My patience is running thin

Need my friend

The hand moves

I want my hand to move with hers

Just thinking about a moment

Missing her smile

Her eyes

Mario Givens

It's like a pause in time

So, I can have my time

To spend with her

Only forever strikes at midnight.

I Miss You

A Dreadful night

My heart stop from the hurt

I know her worth

She defines happiness

With a visual kiss

A moment where I can seize the moment

Hopeless

This is one ride I want to get off

My eyes start to rain

The possibility is insane

I can't believe a dove flew away

Here is where she doesn't stay

I'll continue to pray

Determine if the next chance will be us

So I'll wait

Think

Knock on opportunity door

Who answer

The possibility of rekindling a peaceful life.

Questions

Where do you lead?

Does the ending have peace?

Can I be happy?

Will God hear the words I speak?

Do you suppose to curve?

When will it stop?

Can my vision see?

Why is it dark?

Will negativity flee?

Universe Don't Lie

As I took a flight to Venus

I couldn't believe I seen this

Cupid shot me with an arrow

It penetrated real slow

I pause

Took a glance

I was sitting on the sun

Then I look across the sky

She was sitting on the moon

We begin to make love on the clouds

Then the stars were created

The night ends peacefully

When the universe lives happily ever after pain

I was determined

Shock by the possibility

Inability

To be free from hurt

Pain lives here

Our eyes shed tears

Hearts broken

Insecurity has fears

Only the sun can dry these puddles

Confusion

Emotions creates fights with pain

My shame is the blame

Her feelings are the same

Separation Has arrive

The departure Has landed

It's too severe

The Love didn't survive.

A Shower of Peace

Every drop

It carries peace

A different beat

There's calm to chaos

Relaxation becomes a puddle

Lakes are form

Oceans reminds me of love

I want to dive in

Take A swim to God

Every backstroke

Is an angel protecting his words?

Mario Givens

Free from Hurt

It's not a dream

Reality set In

I'm torn between love and lust

Broken trust

Why did this happen

Can I recover

Life not fair but I discover

I control my heart

The destination is beyond clouds

I don't want pain

Can't deal with shame

Stress don't live here

My soul only has room for good

I won't shed another tear

Dreams don't have nightmares

I just want to sleep

No need to count sheep

Only hearts across my bed is what I see.

A Thought in the Garden

As I think of you

I'm convince you are an angel

Someone who bless my space

My eyes create peace with every blink

My ears can hear your wings flap

You come to me with sincerity

Your spirit has a halo around your heart

There's calm in the air when you fly

The birds chirp

The butterfly's lands on flowers

The trees remain quiet

They recognize a creation

Making of eternity

You kiss me with motivation

A touch of inspiration

Your eyes shine to where the glow

Ease my anticipation.

A Nice Horseback Ride

I just want my chance

Your strength can hold me

Just a day to ride

Release these thoughts

Just me and you

I rub your hair

Hug you close

Letting you know I care

We begin this journey

It started off bumpy and rocky

Then it became smooth

The air blows in my face

I'm so relax

So I stop and give you a treat

You seem happy

I'm happy

I discuss how wonderful you are
You give me a head shake
Then we begin to take the ride home
I dread the moment when the day is over.

Mario Givens

Truthful Skies

As the moon overlooks the clouds

The shapes show perfection

The sky tells the truth

Allowing the world to notice

The universe never lies

Motivating Tulips

Beautiful

Only the earth can kiss your stem

Place in a perfect garden

The sun shines its rays on your bulbs

You have inner light

Your glow brightens the darkest dirt

The roots form more beauty

My day will becomes bless

Once I place you in a vase

Then showcase you in my special place.

Inspiring Good Morning

Hello

May I help you to love?

Maybe a day of happiness

Can I see your smile?

I adore your glow

The possibility of gratification

Your positive energy shows

Then Your eyes say Good day

I can feel your spirit pray

It's my pleasure to meet you

Melancholy becomes satisfied

My moments from a hello

It gives someone hope.

Air

I need you

Not having you cause sadness

I can't breathe

I'm in need

Why can't this feeling leave

Internal grieve

My heart dies

The tears run

Their destination is a puddle of hurt

I need you

The thoughts of glory

An opportunity to smile

Then the pain comes again

My only friend

You give me oxygen

Every breath comes from your love

I blow out slowly

Reminding me you may return

I can't live without you.

Mario Givens

A Day of Hurt

It hurts so bad

My tears have tears

As the water hugs my cheeks

My pain is at its peak

Determine to live

My soul is weak

So hurt

Devastated

The puddles get bigger

The water runs

Creating a lake on my face

My eyes bleeds sorrow

I have a headache

The only medicine is my heart

It will get better tomorrow

Tonight, I suffer

Cupid was sad

He shot me with an arrow

The point has struck me.

Love Died

You can only try

Create a thought to maximize your heart

Be sincere in the war of love

Here lies a heart that's died

Can't pump no more love

Lack of longevity of CPR

The breath of fresh air is polluted

Diluted

Attack by deceitful smog

My loyal respiratory system is clog.

Silent destiny

Destiny made love to failures

Confusion became lust

Temptation decided to leave

Honor don't trust

It creates a vision to form a thought

Deceit is a heartbreak

My soul is silent

My spirit is full of life

The angels descend through the night

The protection of the sky

Mesmerize by the stars

The clouds shadow the moon

The lake has a glare from her rays

Her strength is the power of the waves.

Hello

It's a beautiful night

Your smile created a jealousy trait from the moon

Your inspiration came too soon

I decided to share my dream

You read

I was a little scared

Nervous took over me

Anxious for glorification

Your skin reminds me of the clay

God created

Your spirit is like a scripture

My soul prays

Your eyes connected to the words

So my verbs attract your nouns

A chapter started with once upon a time

A paragraph empty from the period

Your sentence ends with my exclamation mark

A story of hello.

Galaxy of Clarity

The nights call me

I answer with sincerity

I need to relax

Continue peace

The moon is bright

It's talking to me

I can't hear the words

So I respond to the stars

Hoping they will let her know

The air is thin

The temperature is calm.

A Careful Gift

Just a moment to think

Opportunities to speak

So I pause

Measuring the knowledge I share

Patient with care

Realizing a rose needs water

And a smile is the sun

Your eyes are the nourishment

So I pause again

Thinking about putting you in a vase

My heart is the table

Your rest on my chest.

A Perfect Creation

He gave me some clay

I mold her into perfection

Her beauty I carefully touch

Caressing her cheeks

My hands slowly rub both sides of her neck

It takes precision to create her lips

So when she speaks

The roar from her voice

Makes the earth shiver

I just want to give her

An opportunity

Life

Motivation.

Mysterious Thoughts

You are so mysterious

Your calm creates chaos in my mind

Trying to figure your heart

What drives you

Motivates a specimen of beauty

Your eyes tell stories

Your smile reminds me of the sun

When he winks at the moon

The light you possessed

Want to get to know you soon

I want to whisper words in your ears

Each verb brings you near

I hug your spirit

Your soul is safe in my arms

I won't do no harm

I want to be the peace to your storm

The beat to your moan

So who are you miss mystery

Mario Givens

What's on your mind

Can I get closer

Rub my fingers in your hair

Want to be your headband

I want to be near your thoughts

That way when we connect

Our mental stimulation

Forms a bond of ecstasy.

You Are Everywhere

Sitting at the dock

My feet touch the water

All I can do is visual you

Trying to maintain my feelings

It's hard when you miss her

A quick lean back

The sky reminds me of you

The clouds are your hair

So soft

The planes are you

Flying happiness in my heart

The birds display your grace

The moon hides

Like your shyness

At night it glows.

Mario Givens

Forbidden Love

This can't happen

Our emotions got strong

What we are doing is wrong

Started as a kiss

Multiple nights on the phone

Is he home?

I really want to talk

Have a lot on my mind

Wish we could take a walk

Discuss our future of you being mine

This is hard

When all you do is think of her

My feelings are like a raft on the river

The waves take me everywhere

Do you feel the same?

How can we overcome this?

Conquer a destiny that can cause damage

Feelings we must manage

Mindful Thoughts

Many things can be lost

What can we do?

Cloudy thoughts

Leads to miserable faults.

Mario Givens

Ocean

The depth

It possesses many levels

The possibilities

Opportunities

Freedom comes with every splash

Voices only heard from waves

Echoes through the caves

Letters remain hidden in bottles

A dolphin sings melodies

A verse from the octopus strokes

Dancing are the fish and jellies

Sharks command the stage

Moving throughout the concert

Like the security of the sea

The whales move to the water beats

As the Giant squids takes a seat

The sea lions scream from the excitement

In the depths of the ocean

Even the fish needs some fun.

Fallen Leaves

As I look at the trees

The leaves represent our ancestors

Each leaf falls means a slave was hung

The disappointments of our present

The roots die

The branches linger without strength

The pressure from ropes holding necks

A culture dies

Our future should've grown

But we are torn

Disrespecting the connection

Between earth and man

So when winter comes

The tree is naked

It will show you all the damage

The trauma from the pain

The bark loses grace

It will wither and become decease

Life of a fallen race.

Thoughts

Many times, I sit by the window

I wonder where the wind will blow

What will be my legacy?

What can I do to get better?

Want to be the best I can be

So I pray

I think

Come to a reality

My life can be great

I can accomplish dreams

I believe in my faith.

Orchids

You are so beautiful

The centerpiece of my heart

A miracle of a room

Your scent relaxes my roughest day

The calm in my spirit

You capture the sun

I can't wait to place you in a vase

Honor you in a special place

You are full of love

The strength you hold

You are a gift from God

Your fertility

Creates love and peace

A sense of refinement

The definition of grace

You are the bouquet of my life.

Forever Queen

As she looks down at the earth

She smiles

The brightness that shines through the clouds

Our World have peace

The support of God

She Keeps the earth at ease

Her smiles are bright and longer

The wind Is calm

The stars are stronger

The wisdom of her position

She educates the skies

A glimpse of love

When the plane flies by

Her soul creates spirit

Her lessons taught

We all had to listen

She defines what beauty really means

The matriarch of our family

She's our Forever Queen.

Sacred Dinner

As I close my eyes

I realize

The moment is hear

The ecstasy is near

I cough because I'm nervous

The inability to hide my fear

Then she walks up

I can hear the words of others

She's beautiful

Her eyes remind me of peace

I'm anxious again

So my heart drop

Just like a plate hitting the ground

Her words utter hello

I respond so calm

We both smile

The wind blows harder

Telling us to relax

Then I proceed to discuss

Mario Givens

Talking about the good in life

She begins her story

The sincerity of the night

The clouds block the moon

The sounds of the city

Our conversations bloom

We both begin to smile

Her glow

My glow

Her easiness

My relaxing flow

It felt like a classic movie

The good guy wins

This can't be the end of the moment

A special place

Having a scared dinner with a beautiful friend.

Tears for Mama

Don't cry

Your eyes are weak

Your pain needs to sleep

Just Ease your mind

Take a minute to think

Process the words you speak

Misery you haven't felt

Please know I'm telling the truth

It's about to get better

I receive a message

I know what to do

So stop crying

Mommy almost here

You can tell her about your day

How excited you are

With all the games you play

So stop crying

the doorbell rings

Mario Givens

A greet at the door

Hugs and kisses

Her soft voice sings

Mommy got her son

They drive off to peace

Made a right turn on love

Now her son pain can go to sleep.

A Dateless Day

Just a warm afternoon

My feet are buried in the sand

The sun was bright

The waves were kissing the shoreline

Then A boat sail by

Then I realize

I miss her

Holding her hand

Looking into her eyes

I just can't understand

A beautiful day

Wishing my beautiful date was here

Then Another boat sails by

I begin to cry

Lost in my emotions

My heart is healing

Devastated by love

My feelings are sad

I decided to leave, I know deep down this date is over.

Mario Givens

Sheltered Hurt

The clouds were her place of sanctuary

She hid there to not show her fears

The skies are turning dark

A sad and gloomy day

Here comes a storm

Now the rain begins to fall.

Scarred Love

I'm wounded

My heart is bleeding

I'm Reaching for some help

I feel like I'm dying inside

My soul cries

Wondering what's next

Scared from the cut in my chest

I'm Devastated from the lack of love

Stuck between ravens and doves

Can this hurt stop

Please I need a truce

I'll wave the white flag

Let's end this mutual abuse.

A Praying Star

Before you go to sleep young lad

Say a prayer for your life

A prayer for your love ones

Let your words be sincere

Honor thy father

Honor thy mother

Then the night will be calm

Causing a togetherness of love

Families are warm

Security from the deceit of the night.

Happier Feeling

Just be happy

Allow yourself to smile

Enjoy your life

A Rejuvenated feeling

Feels like a child

It's ok to live

Let your journey begin

Have patience with your choices

Make sure your spirit at ease

Getting support from your love ones

Your soul will have forever peace.

Mario Givens

Cupids Arrow

I got lost inside your eyes

They were telling a story

Mystery was the topic

I need to know more

I must figure out why you here

Who sent you

Did Cupid miss his target

The arrow struck me

Created emotions

I want to know your thoughts

Do you think about me?

I wonder do you see what I see

I'm trying to grasp this feeling

It seems to soon

I can't take another love doom

I hope my heart HAs room

Being hurt is not an option

Happy is the ultimate goal

Mindful Thoughts

The root of love

It comes from the honesty soil

Who will water this garden of love?

I'm ready to grow into a flower of peace.

Mario Givens

Appreciation and Gratefulness

Running your bath water

The water is warm

I threw five rose pedals

Each one represents my love for you

I light some candles

The lights are sleep

I place you in the bath

Then I pour you a glass of wine

Slow music plays the background

Close your eyes

Relax your soul

I'll wash your back and feet

A soft kiss on the cheek

I love you

Adore your patience

Appreciate your heart

I take you out the bath

Here's a towel

Mindful Thoughts

Your body is dry
A slow walk into the room
More candles light the mood
I place you on your stomach
Drops of oil consume your back
My hands penetrate peace
Your moan thanks you
She accepts my strength
Her eyes close for the night
A hard day ends with gratitude
I'm blessed to celebrate my love.

www.ingramcontent.com/pod-product-compliance
Lightning Source LLC
Chambersburg PA
CBHW072047290426
44110CB00014B/1587